# STICKER ACTIVITY™

# Bible

## How to play Sticker Activity™

Find the coordinating stickers in the back of the book by page number to complete each activity. Have an adult help you remove the stickers.

Louis Weber, CEO
Publications International, Ltd.
8140 Lehigh Ave
Morton Grove, IL 60053

Illustrated by Stacy Peterson
Additional images from Shutterstock.com

Permission is never granted for commercial purposes.

ISBN: 978-1-64558-727-9

Manufactured in China.

**Keep learning!**
Visit us at littlegrasshopperbooks.com and pilbooks.com

**Follow us!**
 @little.grasshopper.books
@publications_international

 @publications_international
@braingames.tm

Publications International, Ltd.

# Creation

Add stickers to fill God's creation.

God created the whole world. He made the water, sky, and land. God covered the earth with plants and animals.

# Adam Names the Animals

Find the name stickers that match the animal pictures.

Next God made Adam, the first man. God asked Adam to name all the animals.

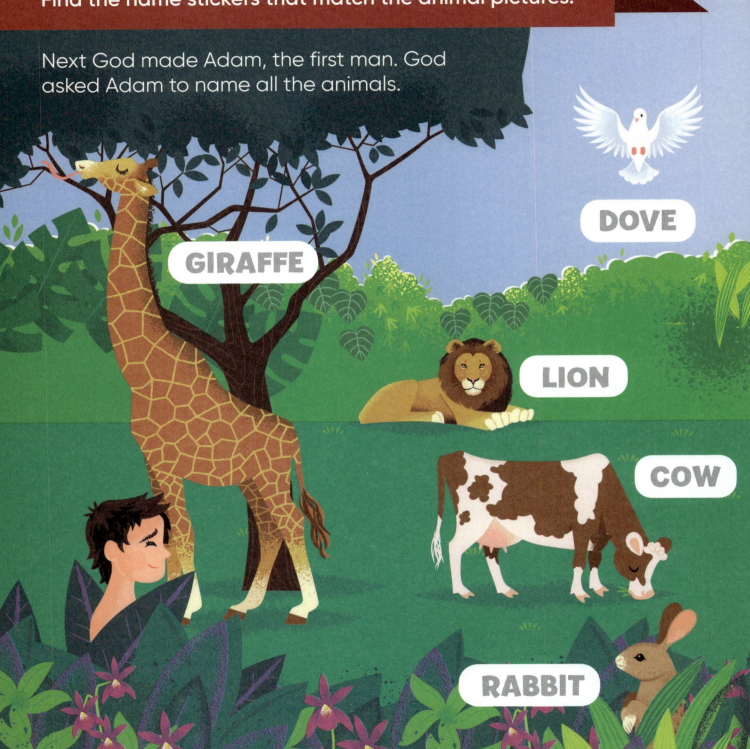

DOVE

GIRAFFE

LION

COW

RABBIT

# Garden of Eden

**Add 6 apples to the tree.**

Then God made the first woman, Eve. Adam and Eve lived in the Garden of Eden. They promised not to eat the fruit from one special tree.

# Noah's Ark

Find the matching pair of each animal.

God told Noah to build a big boat called an ark. He told Noah to bring two of every animal on the ark.

# Joseph's Colorful Coat

Place the sticker with the matching number onto the correct space to complete Joseph's coat.

Joseph's father gave him a colorful coat. This made his brothers jealous. Joseph's brothers sold him to merchants going to Egypt.

Use stickers to finish the patterns.

In Egypt, Joseph became an important person. He helped the Pharaoh make sure there was enough food for everyone to eat. Joseph even gave his brothers food.

# Baby Moses

Add reeds and cattails to help hide baby Moses.

To save her baby brother, Miriam put Moses in a basket. She hid the basket in the river.

# Moses Grows Up

Add stickers to finish the pictures showing how Moses grew up.

The Pharaoh's daughter found baby Moses and raised him as a prince. When he grew up, God spoke to Moses through a burning bush.

# 10 Commandments

Add numbers 1 through 10 next to the commandments.

○ Worship only God.

○ Don't worship idols.

○ Respect God's name.

○ Keep the Sabbath day holy.

○ Respect your parents.

○ Don't hurt others.

○ Be faithful.

○ Don't steal.

○ Tell the truth.

○ Don't be jealous.

God gave Moses 10 commandments for his people to live by.

Add the stickers that match the words.

frogs

grasshoppers

hail

flies

Moses told the Pharaoh to let God's people go. But the Pharaoh said no. So God sent plagues of frogs, flies, hail, and grasshoppers as punishment.

# Exodus

Find these items: 3 chicks, 2 sheep, 2 bluebirds, red hen, Moses, donkey, camel, moon. Place a sticker on each one you find.

After the worst plague, the Pharaoh finally let God's people go. Moses led them out of Egypt to safety.

# David and Goliath

Look at the pictures. Add numbers to show the order they happened.

David visited his brothers. A giant enemy named Goliath challenged someone to fight. Everyone was scared, but not David. With a slingshot and stone, David knocked Goliath down. Everyone cheered for David.

# David's Armor

Place the sticker with the matching number onto the correct space to complete David's armor.

The king gave David a sword and armor to protect him. But the armor was too big. David fought Goliath without armor.

# Daniel and the Lions

Add the missing puzzle pieces to finish the picture.

A new law said everyone must pray to the king instead of to God. Daniel still prayed to God. The king threw Daniel into the lions' den for breaking the law. God sent an angel to keep Daniel safe.

Find the stickers that match the words.

king

angel

candle

soldier

lion

# Jonah and the Whale

Add stickers to the whale's belly.

Jonah was thrown overboard during a big storm at sea. A giant whale swallowed him whole. Jonah prayed for God's help. After three days, the whale spat Jonah out.

# Jesus Is Born

Find these items in the nativity scene: 3 shepherds, 3 gifts, 2 sheep, baby Jesus, donkey, star. Place a sticker on each one you find.

There was no room at the inn, so Mary and Joseph stayed in a stable. Jesus was born that night. A bright star shone overhead. Shepherds visited Jesus. Wise men brought gifts.

# Disciples Match

Find stickers of the disciples' names and add them to the pictures.

When Jesus grew up, he spread the Word of God. Jesus chose 12 helpers, or disciples.

**Peter**

Jesus called Peter his "rock." Peter was one of his best friends and closest disciples.

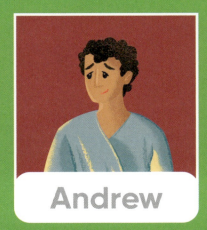

**Andrew**

Andrew and his brother, Peter, were fishermen. Jesus said to them, "Come, I will make you fishers of people."

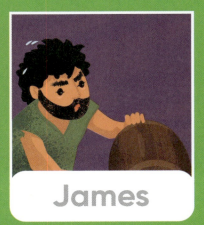

**James**

James was one of Jesus's three main disciples, along with Peter and John.

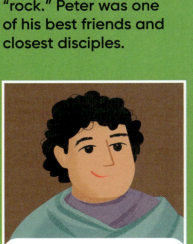

**John**

Like several other disciples, John was a fisherman before Jesus called him.

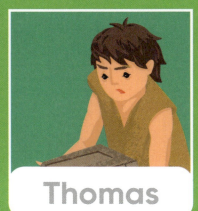

**Thomas**

Thomas was a disciple of Jesus. Thomas once doubted that Jesus rose from the dead.

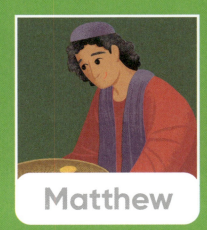

**Matthew**

Matthew was a tax collector before he became a disciple of Jesus.

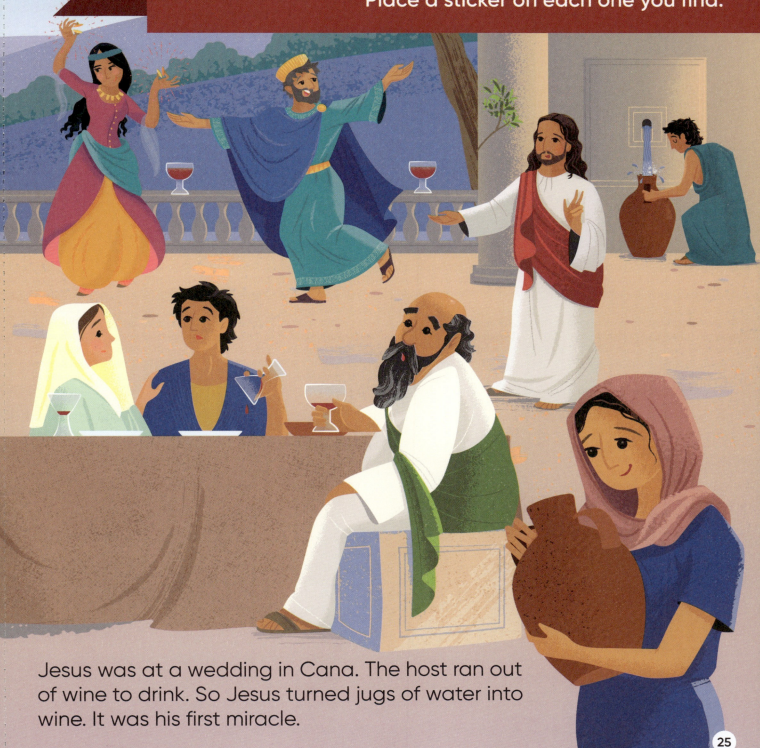

# Miracle at Cana

Find these items: 5 wineglasses, 2 jugs, 2 guests.
Place a sticker on each one you find.

Jesus was at a wedding in Cana. The host ran out of wine to drink. So Jesus turned jugs of water into wine. It was his first miracle.

# Calming the Storm

Add the missing words and stickers to finish the pictures.

storm

boat

Jesus slept on a boat during a storm. His disciples woke him. Jesus calmed the storm.

cloud

calm

sun

miracle

# Loaves and Fishes

Add bread and fish stickers to help Jesus feed the crowd.

One time, a crowd of 5,000 people gathered to hear Jesus teach about God. Jesus changed a few loaves of bread and fish a boy gave him into enough food for everyone.

# The Good Samaritan

Thieves beat up a man and stole his money. Others passed by without helping. Then a Samaritan took the hurt man to an inn and cared for him all night.

# The Lost Sheep

Add 8 sheep to the picture.

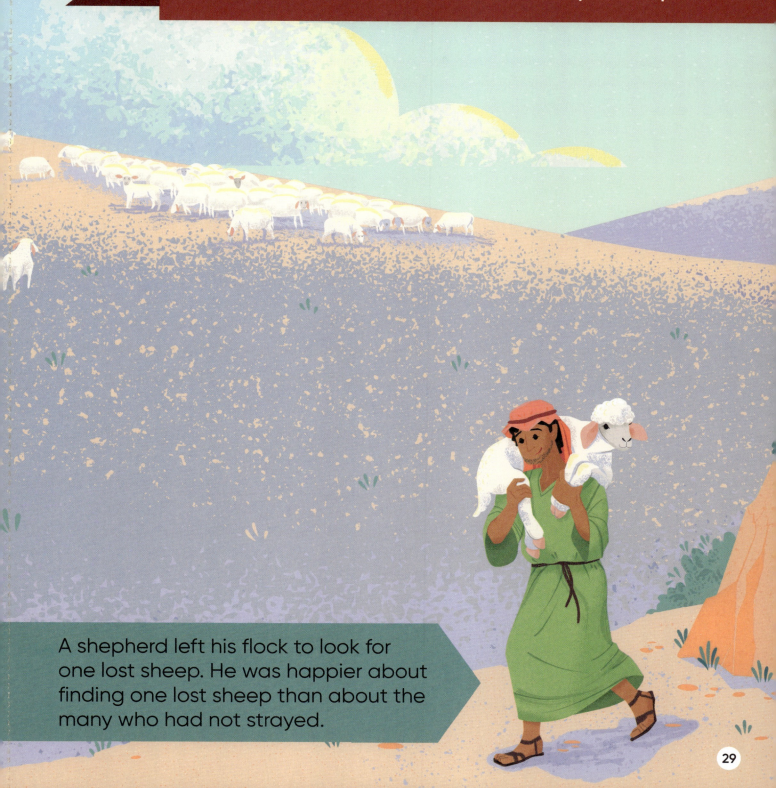

A shepherd left his flock to look for one lost sheep. He was happier about finding one lost sheep than about the many who had not strayed.

# The Prodigal Son

Look at the pictures. Add numbers to show the order they happened.

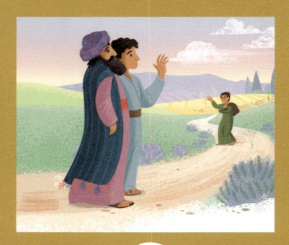

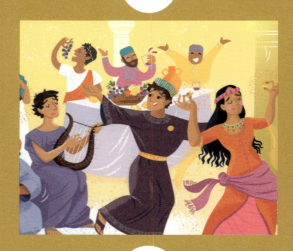

A son moved away from home. He wasted money on wild parties. The only job he could find was feeding pigs. The young man asked his father for forgiveness. His father welcomed him home.

# The Mustard Seed

Find these items: 4 leaves, 3 flowers, bird.
Place a sticker on each one you find.

Jesus said God's kingdom is like a tiny mustard seed that grows into a giant plant. Little things can become big things with God's help.

# Bible Heroes Match

Find the name stickers and add them to the pictures.

## Moses

Moses was a prophet, leader, and teacher. He freed God's people from slavery in Egypt.

## Esther

Esther was a beautiful queen. She saved the Jewish people in Persia.

## Job

Job was a good person. God and Satan tested him. Job stayed faithful to God.

## Deborah

Deborah was a leader, judge, and prophet. She helped her people win a battle.

## Jesus

Jesus was God's son. He taught people how to treat each other and to love God.

## Paul

Paul was a leader in the early Christian church. He traveled to teach people about Jesus.

GIRAFFE

DOVE

LION

COW

RABBIT

P. 4

P. 2-3

P. 5

P. 6-7

1

3

4

2

P. 8

P. 9

P. 10

P. 11

P. 13

P. 12

1
2
3
4
5
6
7
8
9
10

P. 14-15

P. 16

1

2

3

4

1

3

2

4

P. 17

P. 18

P. 19

P. 20-21

P. 22-23

Peter

Thomas

Matthew

Andrew

James

John

P. 24

P. 25

storm    calm

miracle    sun

cloud    boat

P. 26

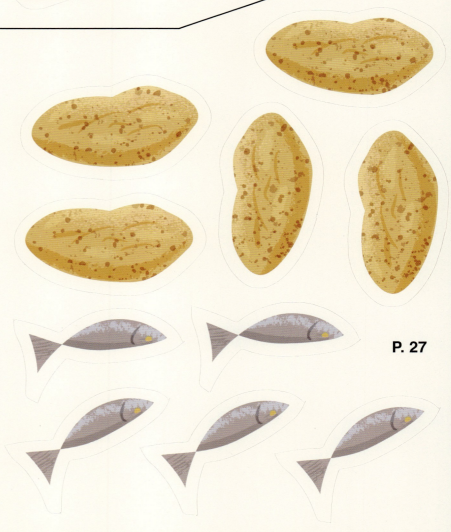

P. 27

1   3

2   4

Job

Jesus

Moses

Esther

Paul

Deborah

# Bonus Stickers